THE *Dogs'* BOOK OF *Romance*

D1546207

Other Books by Kate Ledger and Lisa Sachs

The Cats' Book of Romance

THE *Dogs'* BOOK OF *Romance*

By Kate Ledger

Photography by Lisa Sachs

**Andrews McMeel
Publishing**

Kansas City

The Dogs' Book of Romance

05 06 07 08 09 LEO 10 9 8 7 6 5 4 3 2 1

ISBN-13: 978-0-7407-5481-4
ISBN-10: 0-7407-5481-5

Library of Congress Control Number: 2005924863

www.andrewsmcmeel.com

—— **Attention: Schools and Businesses** ——

Andrews McMeel books are available at quantity discounts with bulk
purchase for educational, business, or sales promotional use. For infor-
mation, please write to: Special Sales Department, Andrews McMeel
Publishing, 4520 Main Street, Kansas City, Missouri 64111.

This, too, for Ben and Jonny

*D*eclare your affection.

Go to the ends of the earth for each other.

Size doesn't matter.

*C*onfide your
deepest secrets.

$\mathcal{L}$earn to appreciate
each other's music.

*K*eep telling the story of how you met.

Plan Sunday brunch
for two.

$\mathcal{L}$eave old relationships
in the past.

*C*herish every
moment together.

*L*ove as though
you're worthy of being loved.

Give from your soul.

*C*ompliment each other
in public.

*S*educe with your
bedroom eyes.

Laugh at each other's jokes.

Steal a kiss.

Meet halfway.

*C*hoose your words carefully during an argument.

Friendship is the heart
of all lasting romances.

See the other point of view.

Dream freely side by side.

$\mathcal{M}$aintain your
sense of humor.

*F*orgive and forget.

Wake one another
to catch the sunrise.

*S*mall gestures speak volumes.

Stay awake for pillow talk.

Intimacy begins when you
let down your guard.

Don't stray.

Share a wish
on a shooting star.

*F*all in love all over again.

Featuring